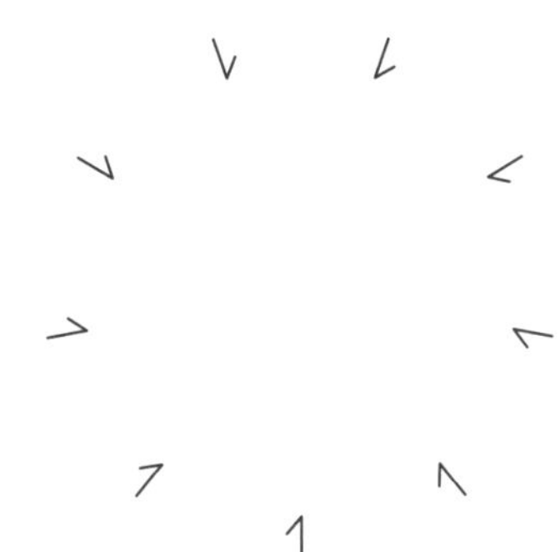

The Witness Practice

A Four-Session Guide to Bear Witness to the Good News of Jesus in Our Cultural Moment

WaterBrook

John Mark Comer and Practicing the Way

WaterBrook

An imprint of the Penguin Random House Christian Publishing Group, a division of Penguin Random House LLC

1745 Broadway, New York, NY 10019

waterbrookmultnomah.com
penguinrandomhouse.com

A WaterBrook Trade Paperback Original

Published in association with Yates & Yates, www.yates2.com.

All photos courtesy of Practicing the Way.

Trade Paperback ISBN 978-0-593-60341-3
Ebook ISBN 978-0-593-60342-0

Printed in the United States of America

1st Printing

The authorized representative in the EU for product safety and compliance is Penguin Random House Ireland, Morrison Chambers, 32 Nassau Street, Dublin D02 YH68, Ireland. https://eu-contact.penguin.ie

BOOKMAKING TEAM: Production editor: Laura Wright • Managing editor: Julia Wallace • Production manager: Linnea Knollmueller

Book and cover design by Practicing the Way

For details on special quantity discounts for bulk purchases, contact specialmarketscms@penguinrandomhouse.com.

Contents

PART 01

Getting Started

Welcome

There is an unspoken principle that we all intuitively live by: Good news is meant to be shared. Consider for a moment—what is usually the very first thing we do with good news like landing a new job, getting into the college we wanted, or discovering an incredible restaurant? Naturally, we want to share it with others—*especially* those closest to us. Yet, for many of us, this isn't always our felt experience with our own faith, and for good reason.

Every day, we are being bombarded with signals from our surrounding culture to "keep our beliefs to ourselves." There is a pronounced allergy—even hostility—in the post-Christian West toward any claims of capital T truth. In our time, it might be acceptable to believe a particular way of life is best for *you,* but it's problematic to suggest that way of life is best for *everyone.* This can all lead to a very private way of following Jesus that, in belief, is "good news for all people" but in practice, just becomes "good news for *me.*" Yet, in the midst of this, Jesus' invitation to witness to him has not expired—it remains just as relevant to modern apprentices as it was to its original hearers. For the last two millennia, followers of Jesus have dared to ask the question: How do we witness to the good news of Jesus in *this* particular moment? Through this Practice, we want to explore that same question for our time.

Over the next several weeks, we will set aside time to explore how Jesus himself entered into witness—his mission, motivation, and method for sharing the good news—to see our compassion grow for the lost, to extend relationship around our tables, and to form words and a way of life in community that witness to the gospel. Now, this kind of witness will not just happen—it will require risk and take practice. But if we say *yes* to this way of relating to the gospel and those around us, we can experience the deep life in Jesus that can only truly be discovered when we generously share it with others.

Welcome to the Practice of Witness.

The Nine Practices

Witness is just one of nine core Practices in the body of resources available from Practicing the Way. The Practices are spiritual disciplines centered around the life rhythms of Jesus. They are designed not to add even more to your already overbusy life, but to slow you down and create space for the Spirit of God to form you to be with Jesus, become like him, and do what he did. Ultimately, they are a way to experience the love of God.

To run another Practice or learn more, turn to page 102.

How to Use This Guide

A few things you need to know

This Practice is designed to be done in community, whether with a few friends around a table, your small group, in a larger class format, or with your entire church.

The Practice is four sessions long. We recommend meeting together every week or every other week. For those of you who want to spend more time on this Practice, we've included an additional four weeks of material in the appendix to go deeper into Scripture and discussion. You are welcome to pause for these studies in between sessions or skip over them.

You will all need a copy of this Companion Guide. You can purchase a print or ebook version from your preferred retailer or find a free digital PDF version at launch.practicingtheway.org. We recommend the print version so you can stay away from your devices during the Practices, as well as take notes during each session. But we realize that digital works better for some.

Each session should take about one to two hours, depending on how long you allow for discussion and whether or not you begin with a meal. See the sample session on the following page.

Are you a group leader or facilitator? Log in to your online Dashboard or sign up at launch.practicingtheway.org to find ideas, best practices, and tips on running this Practice. Page 106 also offers helpful information and tips on running this Practice.

Our Practices are designed to work in a variety of group sizes and environments. For that reason, your gatherings may include additional elements like a meal or worship time, or follow a structure slightly different from this sample. Please adapt as you see fit.

Sample Session

Here is what a typical session could look like.

Welcome

Welcome the group and open in prayer.

Introduction (2–3 min.)

Watch the introduction to the session and pause the video when indicated for your first discussion.

Discussion 01: Practice reflection in triads (15–20 min.)

Process your previous week's spiritual exercise in smaller groups of three to five people with the questions in the Guide.

Teaching (20 min.)

Watch the teaching portion of the video.

Discussion 02: Group conversation (15–30 min.)

Pause the video when indicated for a group-wide conversation.

Testimony and tutorial (5–10 min.)

Watch the rest of the video.

Prayer to close

Close by praying the liturgy in the Guide, or however you choose.

The Weekly Rhythm

The four sessions of this Practice are designed to follow a four-part rhythm that is based on our model of spiritual formation.

01 Learn

Gather together as a community for an interactive experience of learning about the Way of Jesus through teaching, storytelling, and discussion. Bring your Guide to the session and follow along.

02 Practice

On your own, before the next session, go and "put it into practice," as Jesus himself said.* We will provide weekly spiritual exercises to integrate this practice into your everyday life, as well as recommended resources to go deeper.

03 Reflect

Reflection is key to spiritual formation. After your practice and before the next session, set aside 10—15 minutes to reflect on your experience. Reflection questions are included in this Guide at the end of each session.

04 Process together

When you come back together, watch the introduction and then start by sharing your reflections with your group. This moment is crucial, because we need each other to process our life before God and make sense of our stories. If you are meeting in a larger group, you will need to break into smaller subgroups for this conversation so everyone has a chance to share.

---

* Philippians 4v9

Tips on Beginning a New Practice

This Guide is full of spiritual exercises, time-tested strategies, and good advice on the spiritual discipline of witness.

But it's important to note that the Practices are not formulaic. We can't use them to control our spiritual formation, or even our relationship with God. Sometimes they don't even work very well. Over the coming weeks, there may be some days when you feel like a channel of God's love to the world around you, and others when you feel awkward and ineffective. That's normal.

The key with the spiritual disciplines is to let go of outcomes and just offer them up to Jesus in love.

Because it's so easy to lose sight of the ultimate aim of a Practice, here are a few tips to keep in mind as you begin practicing witness.

01 Start small

Start where you are, not where you "should" be. It's counterintuitive, but the smaller the start, the better chance you have of really sticking to it and growing over time. It's better to integrate witness into your life slowly than to commit to an overly ambitious expectation that asks too much of you too soon, and risks burning you out a few weeks in.

02 Think subtraction, not addition

The goal here isn't to add witnessing to your already overbusy, overfull life. You are likely already overwhelmed. Instead, think, *How is God inviting me to witness where I already am?*

Formation is about less, not more—about slowing down and simplifying your life around what matters most: life with Jesus.

03 You get out what you put in

The more fully you give yourself to this Practice, the more life-changing it will be; the more you just dabble with it, the more shortcuts you take, the less of an effect it will have on your transformation.

04 Remember the J curve

Experts on learning tell us that whenever we set out to master a new skill, it tends to follow a J-shaped curve; we often get worse before we get better.

Witness might feel a bit difficult at first; it will get easier over time. Just stay with the Practice.

05 There is no formation without repetition

Spiritual formation is slow, deep, cumulative work that happens over years, not weeks. The goal of this four-week experience is just to get you started on a journey of a lifetime. Upon completion of this Practice, you will have a map for the journey ahead and hopefully some possible companions for the Way.

But what you do next is up to you.

Before You Begin

The following resources are designed to enhance your experience of the Witness Practice, but they are entirely optional.

Recommended reading

Reading a book alongside the Practice can greatly increase your understanding and enjoyment of this discipline. You may love to read, or you may not. For that reason, it's recommended, but certainly not required.

The recommended reading for the Witness Practice is *The Gospel Comes with a House Key* by Rosaria Butterfield. Rosaria is an author, speaker, and former tenured professor of English and women's studies.

The Spiritual Health Reflection

One final note: Before you begin Session 01, please set aside 20—30 minutes and take the Spiritual Health Reflection. This is a self-assessment we developed in partnership with pastors and leading experts in spiritual formation. It's designed to help you reflect on the health of your soul, in order to better name Jesus' invitations to you as you follow the Way.

You can come back to the Spiritual Health Reflection as often as you'd like (we recommend one or two times a year) to chart your growth and continue to move forward on your spiritual journey.

To access the Spiritual Health Reflection, visit practicingtheway.org/reflection and create an account. Answer the prompt questions slowly and prayerfully.

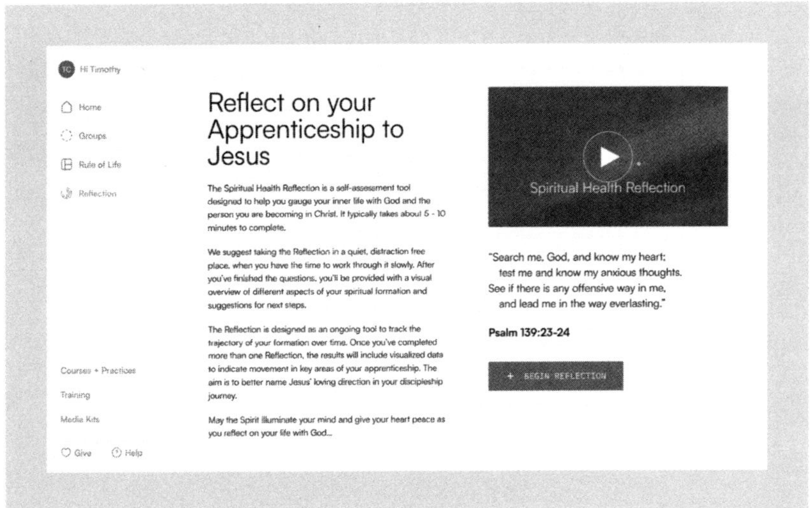

The Practicing the Way primer

If this is your first time engaging with a Practicing the Way resource, we invite you to set aside 15 minutes before Session 01 to watch a primer on spiritual formation. This will give you a brief overview of the *why* behind spiritual practices and key insights to guard and guide your coming practice.

Log in to your online Dashboard, or sign up to watch the primer at launch.practicingtheway.org.

PART 02

The Sessions

SESSION 01

Begin with Love

Overview

Have you ever thought about what needed to happen for you to begin following a Jewish rabbi who lived almost two millennia ago?

Well, somebody *needed* to tell somebody, who *needed* to tell somebody, who *needed* to tell somebody who, at some point in your life, *decided* to tell you about the good news of Jesus.

Our lives in Christ hinge on the practice of witness: where we as apprentices of Jesus open up our lives to others in love, testifying to the good news of Jesus through our words and way of life in community.

And while it's true that we all would not be following Jesus the way we are today without this practice—many of us may also admittedly experience a certain allergic response to the idea of *evangelism*.

It brings up images of uncompassionate preaching on street corners, unsolicited conversations, or perhaps more painfully, well-meaning invitations and interactions that are met with hostility.

But what if our witness to the person of Jesus could be more ordinary and less forced than what we may initially imagine?

And what if the starting place for this practice was not pressure, fear, or obligation, but love?

Opening Questions

When instructed, circle up in triads (smaller groups of three to five people) and discuss the following questions:

01 What brought you to the Witness Practice? What are you hoping to see God do in your life through it?

02 What's your primary feeling about growing as a witness of the life you have found in Jesus? Excitement? Fear? Inadequacy?

03 When you think of what it looks like to share the good news of Jesus to others, what do you initially imagine?

04 Share a moment when you saw or heard someone beautifully share the good news of Jesus through words or deeds with someone who wasn't following him. What made that story memorable for you?

Teaching

Key Scripture

Acts 1v8

Session summary

- Jesus envisions the gospel going out to every corner of the world, *through* our witness.
- Witness is the practice of intentionally opening up our lives to others in love and testifying to the good news of Jesus through our words, and our way of life in community.
- There are five thresholds that Western people cross to become followers of Jesus:

  01 Trusting a Christian

  02 Becoming curious

  03 Opening up to change

  04 Seeking after God

  05 Living in the kingdom*

- The invitation to witness is about loving people wherever they are on this journey.
- Step one is to allow the Spirit of Jesus to grow his compassion for others within our hearts.

---

* Don Everts and Doug Schaupp, *I Once Was Lost: What Postmodern Skeptics Taught Us About Their Path to Jesus* (IVP, 2008).

Teaching Notes

As you watch Session 01 together, feel free to use these pages to take notes.

Discussion Questions

Now it's time for a conversation about the teaching. Pause the video for a few minutes to discuss in small groups:

01 Consider one person who had to be told about Jesus so you could come to know and follow Him. What reflections do you have on that story?

02 What fears or concerns do you have about sharing your faith in our culture?

03 Of the five thresholds Western people typically cross to become followers of Jesus (see Session summary), which most stands out to you, and why?

04 If you were to share your faith today, do you think you would be motivated more by obligation, ambition, or love? How do you hope that motivation will change or be refined throughout this Practice?

Practice Notes

As you continue to watch Session 01 together, feel free to use this page to take notes.

Closing Prayer

Take a few deep breaths, become aware of God's presence, and pray this prayer slowly, leaving short silence between each line.

Father, you have given us your Son,
who so willingly came to us from your heart,
entering our struggle, and laying down his life,
Help us know what it means to love like you,
and to faithfully offer your life, through ours,
to the world around us.

Amen.

Exercise

Identify three to five people you care about who are not followers of Jesus and begin praying for them daily.

We encourage you to write down their names on a small piece of paper, put it in your pocket or somewhere prominent in your home, and then pray for them daily from now to the end of this Practice.

As a part of this exercise, we also invite you to plot those three to five people in the different thresholds shared in this session's teaching. Once you have placed them, ask God to speak to you about the part he is inviting you to play for each particular person.

01 Write down the names of the three to five people here.

Person 01:

Person 02:

Person 03:

Person 04:

Person 05:

02 Place each of those three to five people in the below category that you think best represents where they are in their spiritual journey.

Trusting a Christian

Becoming curious

Opening up to change

Seeking after God

Living in the kingdom

03 Lastly, set aside some time now to ask God to speak to you, in your mind and heart, about what they need to experience next, and what part you play in it. What do you sense needs to happen next in their spiritual journeys to move toward God?

In order to do this, find a quiet space to spend the next 10—15 minutes in prayer:

- To begin, posture yourself how you like to pray and take a few slow, deep breaths, becoming aware of God's loving presence in and around you.
- Bring one of the individuals to your mind, and invite God to speak to you about them. Ask God to reveal where they are at and what they might need to experience next. Listen and note any words or impressions that come to mind.
- Then ask God to show you how you might participate in what he is already doing in their lives. If nothing specific comes to your mind or heart in this step or the one previous, don't worry. Just ask that God would give you more of his compassion for this person, and eyes to see how you can join him in their life.

Repeat the above until you have finished praying for your list of three to five people.

04 Write below what you sensed God speaking and inviting you toward in each person's life. Consider uniquely marking this page with a bookmark or dog-ear, so you can return to your notes below to guide your prayer for these people throughout the Practice.

Person 01:

Person 02:

Person 03:

Person 04:

Person 05:

Reach Exercise

Go on a prayer walk.

Pick an environment you regularly find yourself in; this could be your neighborhood, or a part of town you hang out in, or the area where you work.

As you walk and pray, focus on two things:

01 **Imagining with God:** Try to imagine the spiritual state of people behind the windows and doors and walls. Imagine living without God. Going through divorce or unemployment or bankruptcy or illness, without God or community. Trying to make sense of the universe. Imagine what it would be like to not have a community around you.

02 **Asking of God:** Ask the Spirit of Jesus to give you his heart of compassion for the lost. Invite him to reveal to you how he feels toward the people and scenarios that you imagined throughout your walk.

Our goal with this exercise is just to begin to let God's heart of love arise in our hearts.

Practice Reflection

Reflection is a key component in our spiritual formation.

Millennia ago, King David prayed in Psalm 139v23—24:

> Search me, God, and know my heart;
> test me and know my anxious thoughts.
> See if there is any offensive way in me,
> and lead me in the way everlasting.

South African professor Trevor Hudson has quoted one of his pastoral supervisors as saying, "We do not learn from experience; we learn from reflection upon experience."*

If you want to get the most out of this Practice, you need to do it and then reflect on it.

* Trevor Hudson, *A Mile in My Shoes: Cultivating Compassion* (Upper Room, 2005), 57.

Before your next time together with the group for Session 02, take 10—15 minutes to journal your answers to the following three questions:

01 Where did I feel resistance?

02 Where did I feel joy?

03 Where did I most experience God's nearness?

Note: As you write, be as specific as possible. While bullet points are just fine, if you write your insights out in narrative form, your brain will be able to process them in a more lasting way.

Reflection Notes

Keep Growing (Optional)

The following resources were curated to enhance your experience of this Practice, but they are entirely optional.

Read

The Gospel Comes with a House Key by Rosaria Butterfield (Chapters 01—03)

Listen

Rule of Life podcast on witness (Episode 01)

Bonus Conversation

If you would like to slow down this four-week Practice to give your community more time to sit in each week's teaching and spiritual exercise, you can pause and meet for an optional conversation outlined in the appendix.

SESSION 02

Practice Hospitality

Overview

The table in first-century Israel was more than just a place to eat—it was a symbol of personal identity and social standing.

To eat and drink with someone was to identify with that person as "my people." Sharing a table meant sharing life—and that association had a direct impact on a person's reputation in their community.

This made the table an exclusive place in Jesus' time—a place to mark who was in with you and who was out. For Jesus, however, the table was not a boundary line or a way to fence people out, but a way to invite people into God's community of love.

While our witness should take many shapes and forms, in a post-Christian culture that is often apathetic to, confused about, or at worst hostile to the gospel, our method for joining Jesus in his mission to "seek and to save the lost" must become more about compassionate presence.

How can we bear witness to Jesus in a time like this? In a very ordinary setting—one shared meal at a time, around a table with the lost.

Reflection Questions

When instructed, circle up in triads (smaller groups of three to five people) and discuss the following questions:

01 Share about one of the people you chose to pray for daily. Who is this person, and why have you decided to pray for them regularly?

02 What did you sense God speak to you about what they need to experience, and your part to play in that?

03 If you were to honestly share your level of hope that these people will someday follow Jesus, what would you say? What reflections do you have on your sense of hopefulness?

04 What new attitudes or perspectives do you hope God forms in you over time through this regular prayer?

Teaching

Key Scripture

Luke 19v1—10

Session summary

- The practice of hospitality has the potential to cut through the hostility of our post-Christian culture and open people to God.
- Hospitality was the primary method by which Jesus lived into his mission "to seek and to save the lost."
- Hospitality is expressing the welcome of God the Father to all through tangible acts of love, ideally through giving food, shelter, and relationship.
- The New Testament writers command that we carry on the practice of hospitality from Jesus' life.
- Practicing hospitality starts not by adding yet another thing to our busy schedules, but by opening a seat for our neighbors, co-workers, and friends at the meals we are already eating.

Teaching Notes

As you watch Session 02 together, feel free to use these pages to take notes.

Discussion Questions

Now it's time for a conversation about the teaching. Pause the video for a few minutes to discuss in small groups:

01 What responses have you most often witnessed when people share the gospel of Jesus—hostility, openness, or indifference?

02 Reflect on a time when you experienced "radically ordinary hospitality." What did that look like, and what impact did it have on you?

03 How does the idea of being hospitable to those who don't know Jesus either complement or challenge your view of the practice of witnessing?

04 What do you know about your neighbors? What thoughts or emotions arise when you consider having them over for a meal around your table?

Practice Notes

As you continue to watch Session 02 together, feel free to use this page to take notes.

Closing Prayer

End your time together by praying this liturgy:

Jesus, teach us the way of
your radically ordinary hospitality—
of simple bread and wine—that we
may daily give away the sweetness
of your heart, the comfort of your
love, and the joy of our Father
to this world you long to heal.

Amen.

Exercise

Invite someone to share a meal.

This meal can be in your home; it can be a feast you prepare for them. Or it can be a food cart down the street from your work and a quick lunch with a co-worker.

If at all possible, we recommend sharing this meal in your home. Depending on your living situation, you might not be set up for an invitation like this—and that's okay. Remember, this is about hospitality, not entertainment. Your home doesn't need to be perfect to invite people to your table and your lives.

As you think of a person to invite, aim for someone who meets three criteria:

01 They are in your life—a friend or neighbor or co-worker.

02 You've not had them over before.

03 They are not yet a follower of Jesus.

The Rule of Saint Benedict says that all guests are to be welcomed as Christ. Treat them the way you would treat Christ himself—with honor, love, and service.

For now, unless an opportunity presents itself, don't focus on telling them about Jesus; focus more on listening. Ask as many questions as you can—about their story, their life, their heart, their pain. Move the conversation from the superficial to the spiritual simply through asking great questions.

Here is a list of questions that you can consider asking:

- Where did you grow up, and what did you love about your upbringing? Is there anything you would change about it, or wish was done differently?
- In what ways are you different from who you were when you were young? How are you the same?
- What is one of the significant moments from your life that shaped who you are today?
- Who in your life has had a big impact on you, and the way you see the world? In what way(s)?
- Who are the people and relationships that are most important to you today?
- What are some of the goals that you are currently working toward? What dreams and aspirations do you have?
- When you think of the kind of person that you most want to emulate or become like, who comes to mind?
- What do you believe is the meaning of life?
- What are some of the values/rules that you try to live by? Where did you learn or pick those up?
- If you had to sum up this past year in a few words, what would those words be?
- What aspects of your life are you most encouraged by as of late? Is there anything you are finding especially difficult?
- Do you believe in any kind of God, or have a spirituality you live by? What do you believe and what does that look like for you?

Reach Exercise

Create a neighborhood map.

Use the "Block Map"* to fill out the names and details of your neighbors—as in those who live next door. If you are not able to fill out as much of it as you hoped, then that's your practice for the coming season. Practice hospitality as a way of learning your neighbors' names and stories.

Block Map

The center square is your home or apartment. The eight squares around it are your eight closest neighbors. Do the following for each neighbor:

01 **On line a,** fill in their name. Ideally first and last, but just put down what you know. If you don't know their name yet, put down a question mark, or leave it blank. Do the same for the next two lines.

02 **On line b,** fill in any details about their lives you know that you couldn't get from waving from a distance: where they work, where they are from, how long they've lived there, what they do for fun, etc.

03 **On line c,** see if you can fill in any in-depth information: their dreams for the future, relationship status, faith (or lack of it), experience with God or church, childhood story, or any pain, etc.

---

* This exercise is from *The Art of Neighboring* by Jay Pathak and Dave Runyon. Copyright © 2012. Used by permission of Baker Books, a division of Baker Publishing Group. Discover more at artofneighboring.com.

a. b. c.	a. b. c.	a. b. c.
a. b. c.		a. b. c.
a. b. c.	a. b. c.	a. b. c.

As a general rule, only 10 percent of people can fill in line a, only 3 percent can fill in line b, and less than 1 percent can fill in line c. The point here isn't guilt and shame; it's simply to plot out just how well you know (or don't know) your neighbors, to get you started on the journey to loving them.

Practice Reflection

Before your next time together with the group for Session 03, take 10—15 minutes to journal your answers to the following three questions:

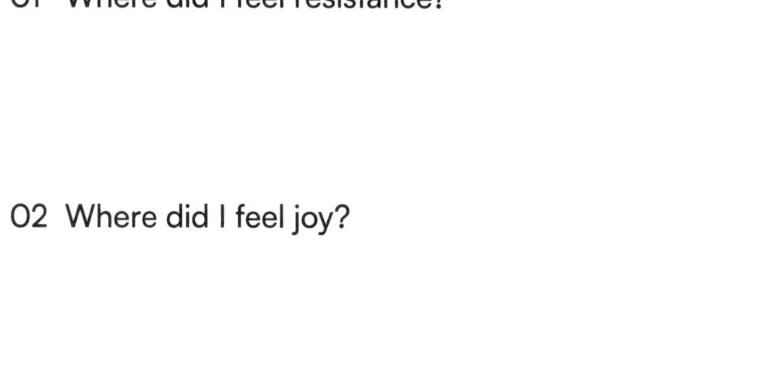

01 Where did I feel resistance?

02 Where did I feel joy?

03 Where did I most experience God's nearness?

Note: As you write, be as specific as possible. While bullet points are just fine, if you write your insights out in narrative form, your brain will be able to process them in a more lasting way.

Reflection Notes

Keep Growing (Optional)

The following resources were curated to enhance your experience of this Practice, but they are entirely optional.

Read

The Gospel Comes with a House Key by Rosaria Butterfield (Chapters 04—06)

Listen

Rule of Life podcast on witness (Episode 02)

Bonus Conversation

If you would like to slow down this four-week Practice to give your community more time to sit in each week's teaching and spiritual exercise, you can pause and meet for an optional conversation outlined in the appendix.

SESSION 03

Partner with the Holy Spirit

Overview

The invitation to witness to the good news of Jesus can give rise to many different emotions—excitement and expectation, but also anxiety and, at times, overwhelm.

Often, that particular feeling of overwhelm can come from thinking, *It is my job to bring God to people.*

Now, if that were true, we would have good reason to feel overwhelmed. But what if the practice of witness isn't about bringing God to people, but about joining Him where He's already at work in a person's life? What if it's about growing in our ability to hear and listen to the Holy Spirit's nudges in our everyday interactions with others?

The most faithful witnesses to Jesus are those who see witness primarily as joining *with* God; they are the ones who regularly pay attention to how he might be gently moving those he loves toward him, and who take the next step in partnership with him.

It's in this kind of partnership that we are able to move beyond reliance on the power of our own capabilities, and into a way of relating to God and others that is filled to the brim with the power of the Holy Spirit.

Reflection Questions

When instructed, circle up in triads (smaller groups of three to five people) and discuss the following questions:

01 Whom did you invite over for a meal this week, and how did they respond? If they said yes and already came over, share what that experience was like.

02 What emotions did you experience before or during the invitation? How about during the meal?

03 What drew you to invite the person you did? What are or were you hoping would happen through this meal?

04 What reflections do you have on ordinary hospitality as a way to share your life in Jesus?

Teaching

Key Scripture

Acts 8v26—39

Session summary

- Our practice of witness is often built on a false assumption that we need to bring God *to* people.
- When we realize God is already at work in all people, our job becomes slowing down and seeing where the Father is already at work, so we can join in.
- From the story of Philip witnessing to the Ethiopian eunuch, we see four movements:

  01 **Listening:** Spending time listening for God's voice and direction

  02 **Looking:** Paying attention and inviting God to give us his eyes for others

  03 **Asking:** Posing a question to start or move the conversation deeper

  04 **Risking:** Taking a practical step of faith to participate in what God is doing in another's life

- As we depend on the person of the Holy Spirit, our witness may take the form of words, or even signs and wonders.
- The starting place of us learning to partner with God's Spirit is to ask, "God, what are you doing? And how do I join in?"

Teaching Notes

As you watch Session 03 together, feel free to use these pages to take notes.

Discussion Questions

Now it's time for a conversation about the teaching. Pause the video for a few minutes to discuss in small groups:

01 How does reframing witness as joining God in what he is already doing, rather than bringing people to him, shift your perspective or approach to sharing Jesus with others?

02 Which of the four movements from the story of Philip and the Ethiopian eunuch do you most want God to strengthen in your life—listening, looking, asking, or risking? Why?

03 What has your experience been like in learning to discern and pay attention to the Holy Spirit's promptings? What are you learning through that process?

04 When was the last time you found yourself in a position where you needed God to show up in power? How did he show up, or how do you wish he had?

Practice Notes

As you continue to watch Session 03 together, feel free to use this page to take notes.

Closing Prayer

End your time together by praying this liturgy:

Help us, Holy Spirit, to live sensitive
to you, to trust you when you speak
and to have the courage to act,
that in our learning to live our lives
in you, we may experience the
power of your love for our world.

Amen.

Exercise

Engage in active listening.

This week, get together with someone who is not a follower of Jesus, and practice listening to them as deeply as you can.

This can be a coffee or a lunch break or a conversation on the porch; it can be scheduled or impromptu, but find at least one time this week to listen.

Follow the SLANT method:

01 **Sit up:** Lean toward them, and be fully engaged.

02 **Look and listen:** Put your phone away, and be fully present.

03 **Ask and answer questions:** You can say things like "Tell me more about . . ." and "How did . . . make you feel?"

04 **Nod your head:** Show them you are engaged through nonverbal communication.

05 **Track the speaker:** Eye contact is very important; track with them for the whole time.

As you listen to them, also listen for where God is already at work in their life.

As they talk, ask the Holy Spirit to show you what he is up to.

But the main goal is just for them to feel loved. As the Mennonite educator David Augsburger put it, "Being heard is so close to being loved that for the average person they are almost indistinguishable."*

---

* David Augsburger, *Caring Enough to Hear and Be Heard* (Regal, 1982), 12.

Reach Exercise

Ask to pray for someone who is not a Christian.

This too could be scheduled or impromptu, but it will likely be unplanned. When you see someone who is sick, or has a need, just gently ask if you could pray for them. Then pause, go slowly, and pray what God puts on your heart.

We put a liturgy below for you to pray daily this week, just asking the Holy Spirit to lead you, and empower you when the moment comes.

As you prepare this week to pray for someone who is not a follower of Jesus, we invite you to pray the following liturgy daily—ideally in the morning before you go into your day.

Find a place quiet and hidden away for 3 minutes each day to prepare your heart for witness through this reflective prayer meditation. To begin, posture yourself how you like for prayer and take a few slow, deep breaths, becoming aware of God's loving presence in and around you.

Then pray:

Father, help me to see every need
around me as a holy opportunity
to reveal your love, to be hospitable,
to speak your Word, to pray for
miracles. In the name of Christ,
the hope of the world.

Amen.

Then, taking just a few minutes, walk through in your mind some of the small but holy opportunities that might present themselves in your day—a conversation with a co-worker, a friend, someone at the shops, at the gym, or your neighborhood where you live.

As you imagine, think about your heart being postured toward witness in God's love. What would that feel like? How would you be listening to God? How might you be bold in introducing them to him or inviting them more into your world?

As you're looking ahead, ask the Spirit for wisdom, love, courage, and compassion to follow him if and when those moments arise.

At the end of this time, you may like to finish with this simple prayer:

Holy Spirit, I am willing.
Help me to see, and act,
in love toward my neighbor.

Amen.

Practice Reflection

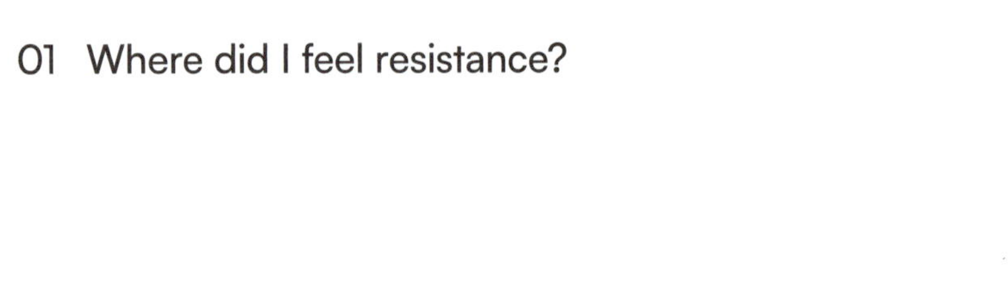

Before your next time together with the group for Session 04, take 10—15 minutes to journal your answers to the following three questions:

01 Where did I feel resistance?

02 Where did I feel joy?

03 Where did I most experience God's nearness?

Note: As you write, be as specific as possible. While bullet points are just fine, if you write your insights out in narrative form, your brain will be able to process them in a more lasting way.

Reflection Notes

Keep Growing (Optional)

The following resources were curated to enhance your experience of this Practice, but they are entirely optional.

Read

The Gospel Comes with a House Key by Rosaria Butterfield (Chapters 07—09)

Listen

Rule of Life podcast on witness (Episode 03)

Bonus Conversation

If you would like to slow down this four-week Practice to give your community more time to sit in each week's teaching and spiritual exercise, you can pause and meet for an optional conversation outlined in the appendix.

SESSION 04

Share the Good News

Overview

Among the words the New Testament writers used to describe followers of Jesus, perhaps none hit quite so close to home as the apostle Peter's description: "foreigners and exiles."

Walk the streets of most cities in the post-Christian West as a follower of Jesus, and you're likely to feel the force of those words—this sense that you don't quite "belong" in the surrounding culture; you're a kind of spiritual refugee.

For many of us, that feeling can turn our faith into, at best, an awkward conversation and, at worst, a personal hobby we would rather hide away.

In the midst of that very real experience, it can be helpful to remember that the gospel is *good news*. And while there are those who will be turned off by it, others' hearts might leap to believe it. They might even say, "Why didn't you tell me this sooner?"

Because, after all, it's "good news . . . for all the people."*

Jesus invites us to both show *and* tell this good news—for our deeds and our words to testify to the beauty of the life we have in him.

---

* Luke 2v10

Reflection Questions

When instructed, circle up in triads (smaller groups of three to five people) and discuss the following questions:

01 Share about what you did for this week's exercise—listening actively to someone who is not a follower of Jesus—and what that experience was like.

02 Where did you encounter resistance in yourself as you asked questions and listened?

03 What did you learn about the person that fostered empathy or compassion in you? What reflections do you have on the power of curiosity and listening?

04 What was your experience like in trying to attune yourself both to the person and to God? What did you sense God saying or inviting you toward throughout the conversation?

Teaching

Key Scripture

1 Peter 2v11—12

Session summary

- The practice of witness is about both showing and sharing the good news of Jesus in our everyday lives.
- There are six best practices for witness in our time:
    - **Live a beautiful life in community:** Be a sign of the coming kingdom of God in the way you navigate life and relationships.
    - **Be authentic:** Live relationally and be honest about your faith in Jesus.
    - **Pray:** Remember that someone coming to follow Jesus is primarily a work of the Spirit.
    - **Practice hospitality:** Intentionally make room at your table for the lost.
    - **Tell your story:** Share how your relationship with Jesus has impacted your life.
    - **Share the good news of Jesus:** When the time is right, be prepared to share who Jesus is and what he has done.
- As we join God in this work, we must remember we are not responsible for the outcomes. We are just witnesses.

Teaching Notes

As you watch Session 04 together, feel free to use these pages to take notes.

Discussion Questions

Now it's time for a conversation about the teaching. Pause the video for a few minutes to discuss in small groups:

01 In what ways has following Jesus in our culture felt like being a "foreigner" or "exile" to you?

02 What aspects of your life in Jesus do you consider beautiful and worth inviting others into?

03 Do you tend to want to share the good news of Jesus more through your life or words? Why do you think that is?

04 Consider one of the people you have been praying for daily throughout this Practice. What is God forming in you through prayer? What outcomes are you needing to surrender to him for that person?

Practice Notes

As you continue to watch Session 04 together, feel free to use this page to take notes.

Closing Prayer

End your time together by praying this liturgy:

Jesus Christ, Divine Word, who lived and spoke, and showed us the way, we ask for wisdom and courage that we may, with you, speak this news that has so transformed and healed us—this news of your closeness, your glory and love—that all may come to know, and experience, the beauty of your heart.

Amen.

Exercise

Practice articulating the gospel in your own words.

We're not going to ask you to share the gospel with a non-Christian, unless the right opportunity presents itself; but we are going to ask you to get together with another person from your community, just to get coffee or meet up somewhere easy, and practice verbally speaking the good news of Jesus to each other.

You can role-play a little, but the main goal is to be prepared to share your faith when the right time comes.

Reach Exercise

Identify two to three of the main objections people have against the gospel in your cultural context or relational world.

This is more of an apologetics exercise. But we're not asking you to become an intellectual expert, though that may be God's call on a few of you. We're just asking you to love others by really thinking deeply and well about the major questions people have about God or the Christian Way, and that work as barriers to their coming to faith.

You won't be able to do this in one week; for this week, just identify a few of the main questions people have, and start to hunt for a few good resources to learn more. Then, in the coming season, prepare yourself to "give an answer."*

Take these questions to a trusted pastor or leader in your community, and have them recommend resources to help you form a thoughtful response. You may also go to page 101 to see our Recommended Reading for this Practice. Write the resources below:

* 1 Peter 3v15

Practice Reflection

As you come to the end of this Practice, take 10—15 minutes to journal your answers to the following three questions.

01 Where did I feel resistance?

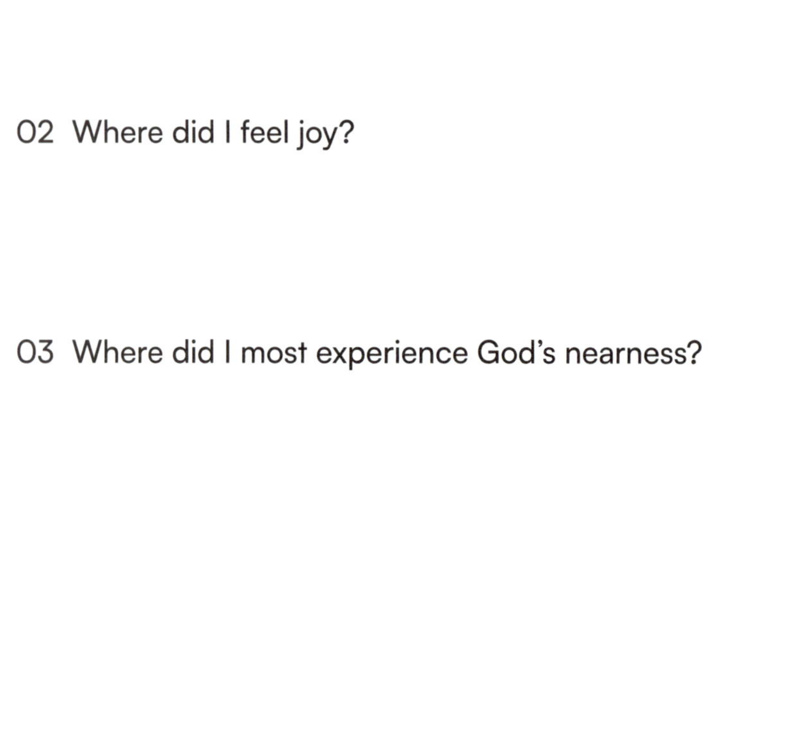

02 Where did I feel joy?

03 Where did I most experience God's nearness?

Note: As you write, be as specific as possible. While bullet points are just fine, if you write your insights out in narrative form, your brain will be able to process them in a more lasting way.

Reflection Notes

Keep Growing (Optional)

The following resources were curated to enhance your experience of this Practice, but they are entirely optional.

Read

The Gospel Comes with a House Key by Rosaria Butterfield (Chapter 10 and Conclusion)

Listen

Rule of Life podcast on witness (Episode 04)

Bonus Conversation

If you would like to slow down this four-week Practice to give your community more time to sit in each week's teaching and spiritual exercise, you can pause and meet for an optional conversation outlined in the appendix.

As you go, may you receive the
power of the Holy Spirit.

May the Spirit of Christ cause
you to be his witnesses—in your
neighborhoods, and communities,
and to the ends of the earth.

And may the beauty of your words,
and your lives, serve as a sign of the
kingdom of God.

PART 03

Continue the Journey

Further Practice

You are not going to explore the full scope of the practice of witness in four weeks. This short Practice is only designed to get you moving on a lifelong journey. You may choose to make witness a rhythmic part of your discipleship, on a weekly or monthly basis, by intentionally continuing to pray for your three to five people, or hosting meals for your neighbors.

Where you go from here is entirely up to you, but if you decide to integrate witness into your life, here's a list of next steps to continue your Practice.

Run Alpha

If you're interested in hosting conversations about Jesus around a table, we highly recommend you run Alpha with your church or community. It can be done in large numbers in a church building or with just a few in your living room or around your dining room table. Over 11 sessions and a retreat, guests are introduced to the person and message of Jesus, and space is created for open, nonjudgmental conversations exploring faith and spirituality.

Learn more by going to alphausa.org/try and finding the Alpha platform in your region.

Recommended Reading

Here are some of our favorite books on the Practice of Witness for those of you who desire to learn more:

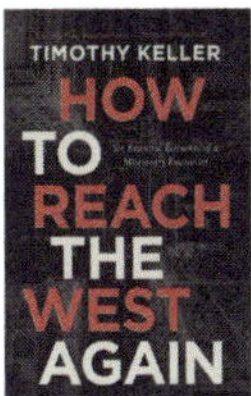

How to Reach the West Again by Timothy Keller

A short, easy-to-read, and absolutely fantastic treatise on the future of witness in the West. It's more conceptual than practical, and geared specifically toward pastors and leaders, but there is wisdom in it for all modern Christians.

I Once Was Lost by Don Everts and Doug Schaupp

The source material for the "five thresholds" from Session 01, these two InterVarsity leaders spent years on the campus of UCLA, and offer their wisdom and insights on our cultural conditions.

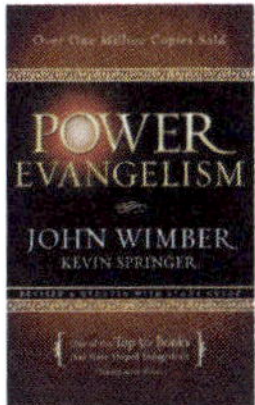

Power Evangelism by John Wimber and Kevin Springer

The go-to book on marrying the practice of preaching the gospel and demonstrating the gospel. A provocative and fascinating call to the New Testament's robust model of evangelism.

The Provocative Church by Graham Tomlin

A compelling vision of a "gospeling" church, based on the New Testament model; written primarily for church leaders and pastors.

Telling Others by Nicky Gumbel

The Alpha companion book, with great stories and best practices for running Alpha in your church or community.

The Practices

Information alone isn't enough to produce transformation.

By adopting not just the teaching but the practices from Jesus' own life, we open up our entire being to God and allow him to transform us into people of love.

Our nine core Practices work together to form a Rule of Life for the modern era.

Sabbath	**Prayer**	**Fasting**
Solitude	**Generosity**	**Scripture**
Community	**Service**	**Witness**

WHAT'S INCLUDED FOR EACH PRACTICE

Four Sessions

Each session includes teaching, guided discussion, and weekly exercises to integrate the Practices into daily life.

Companion Guide

A detailed guide with question prompts, session-by-session exercises, and space to write and reflect.

Recommended Resources

Additional recommended readings and podcasts to get the most out of the Practices.

Learn more by visiting practicingtheway.org/resources.

The Practicing the Way Course

An eight-session primer on spiritual formation.

Two thousand years ago, Jesus said to his disciples, "Follow me." But what does it mean for us to follow Jesus today?

The Practicing the Way Course is an on-ramp to spiritual formation, exploring what it means to follow Jesus and laying the foundation for a life of apprenticeship to him.

WHAT'S INCLUDED

Eight Sessions

John Mark and other voices teaching on apprenticing under Jesus, spiritual formation, healing from sin, meeting God in pain, crafting a Rule of Life, living in community, and more.

Exercises

Weekly practices and exercises to help integrate what you've learned into your everyday life.

Guided Conversations

Prompts to reflect on your experience and process honestly in community.

Companion Guide

A detailed workbook with exercises, space to write and reflect, and suggestions for supplemental resources.

Learn more by visiting practicingtheway.org/resources.

Practicing the Way: *Be with him. Become like him. Do as he did.*

The first followers of Jesus developed a Rule of Life, or habits and practices based on the life of Jesus himself. As they learned to live like their teacher, they became people who made space for God to do his most transformative work in their lives.

Practicing the Way is a vision for the future, shaped by the wisdom of the past. It's an introduction to spiritual formation accessible to both beginners and lifelong followers of Jesus, and a companion to the Practicing the Way Course (practicingtheway.org/course). This book offers theological substance, astute cultural insight, and practical wisdom for creating a Rule of Life in the modern age.

You can order your copy or get copies for your community at practicingtheway.org/book or through your preferred bookseller.

The Circle

Practicing the Way is a nonprofit that develops spiritual formation resources for churches and small groups learning how to become apprentices in the Way of Jesus.

We believe one of the greatest needs of our time is for people to discover how to become lifelong disciples of Jesus. To that end, we help people learn how to be with Jesus, become like him, and do as he did, through the practices and rhythms he and his earliest followers lived by.

All of our downloadable ministry resources are available at no cost, thanks to the generosity of The Circle and other givers from around the world who partner with us to see formation integrated into the church at large.

To learn more or join us, visit practicingtheway.org/give.

For Facilitators

Before you begin, there are three easy things you need to do (this should take only 10—15 minutes).

01 Go to launch.practicingtheway.org, log in, create a group, and send a digital invitation to your community. This will give your group access to the Spiritual Health Reflection, videos, and all sorts of valuable extras. Encourage your group to bring along their Companion Guides to each session, as these contain the discussion questions and space to take notes.

- You can purchase a print or ebook version from your preferred retailer or find a free digital PDF version at launch.practicingtheway.org. We recommend the print version so you can stay away from your devices during the Practices, as well as take notes during each session. But we realize that digital works better for some.
- Note: You can order the Guides ahead of time and have them waiting when people arrive for Session 01, or encourage people to order or download their own and bring them to your gatherings.

02 Send a message to your group encouraging everyone to take the Spiritual Health Reflection before your first gathering. You can direct your group to practicingtheway.org/reflection.

03 If your group has not been through the Practicing the Way Course, invite them to watch this short primer in the online Dashboard before you gather for Session 01 of this Practice.

For training, tips, and more resources for facilitating the Witness Practice, log in to the Dashboard at launch.practicingtheway.org.

APPENDIX

Bonus Conversations

For those of you who want to spend longer sitting in this Practice, we've included an additional four weeks of material in this Guide to go deeper in Scripture and discussion.

You are welcome to pause in between sessions for these additional conversations or skip over them.

Begin with Love

The word *compassion* emerges all throughout Scripture—especially as a way to describe God. The Gospels, in particular, make it abundantly clear that every sign of the kingdom of heaven brought about by Jesus—every opened eye, demon cast out, and meal shared with a stranger—was motivated by compassion. In today's passage, we see Jesus' mission to proclaim the good news of the kingdom through words and deeds, side by side with his motivation: not duty, but sincere love. And ultimately, we see his desire for us to make his mission and motivation our own.

Read Matthew 9v35—38.

Discuss the Scripture

01 Prior to following Jesus, in what ways did you feel most "helpless" or "like [a] sheep without a shepherd"? Try to remember and describe what life was like without God.

02 Jesus had compassion on the crowds. What needs in the lives of those around you who don't know Jesus most engage your sense of compassion?

03 Do you believe that "the harvest is plentiful" in your immediate world today? Why or why not?

04 What do you notice tends to hold you back from being one of the "few" workers being sent out into the harvest? What do you feel you need from Jesus in order to join him in that work?

Discuss the practice

01 What have you been specifically praying for your three to five people in the last couple weeks? Are there any new attitudes or perspectives you're seeing God form in you as you pray?

02 Thinking about just one of these people specifically, what do you sense is your part to play in their current spiritual journey? How is that going so far?

03 How has praying for these individuals impacted or changed your interactions with them?

04 Who on your list do you have the hardest time believing could enter life in the kingdom? What do you think God might be saying or inviting you into through that relationship specifically?

Repeat the exercise

For this week, we invite you to repeat the exercise on page 30 or to try the reach exercise there if you have not already.

Practice Hospitality

Simon the Pharisee's table was an exclusive place—mostly a stage to show off his high social standing. In that world, and in most homes in first-century Israel, there was no such thing as an "open invite." Yet, in this story, we see three people who would never sit together (if not for Jesus)—all at the same meal. And it's Jesus' response to Simon that begs us to consider not just how we will use our tables, but who we are or aren't willing to invite to them.

Read Luke 7v36—43.

Discuss the Scripture

01 What about this story stands out to you, or do you find compelling?

02 What do you think Simon the Pharisee judged "correctly" according to Jesus, and what did he previously judge incorrectly about Jesus and this woman?

03 How does Jesus' willingness to forgive debt, regardless of the apparent size, impact how you see the people in your life who aren't currently following him?

04 How do you currently use your home and table as it relates to this practice, and in what ways do you feel challenged or invited through a story like this?

Discuss the practice

01 Share about this past week's exercise. How did you go about inviting the person you did to a meal, and what did your time around the table look like?

02 How would you describe the connection you were able to establish over the meal? What were you initially expecting?

03 In what ways does this form of witnessing feel more accessible or challenging to you?

04 What would it take for you to make this kind of hosting a part of your regular rhythm? What could that look like?

Repeat the exercise

For this week, we invite you to repeat the exercise on page 52 or to try the reach exercise there if you have not already.

Partner with the Holy Spirit

There is a common lie we can believe that the moments we risk in witness to others depend on our own capabilities—that if we just have the *right* words and the *right* delivery, *then* people will believe. But Paul suggests something different in this passage—that the real power isn't found in ourselves, but in *who* we partner with: God himself. And that there is a way for people to discover the life with God that rests beyond argument and persuasion, and on the living God himself.

Read 1 Corinthians 2v1—5.

Discuss the Scripture

01 What stories of witnessing do you know of, whether personally or not, where it involved a demonstration of God's power?

02 Take note of what Paul actively chose to avoid as he witnessed to the people of Corinth. How does this way of witnessing confront or challenge your understanding or experience of witnessing?

03 What comfort do you take in Paul describing his witness to the Corinthian people as "in weakness with great fear and trembling"? How does this compare to your own experience?

04 In what areas of your witness to others do you feel weak or incapable? How might these areas be invitations to depend on God, and for him to demonstrate his power?

Discuss the practice

01 Share about what this week's exercise looked like for you, and how it went.

02 It's been said that the feeling of being listened to and loved are very similar for the average person. How have you experienced this personally?

03 What did you notice happen as you tried to attune yourself to the person and to God in the moment? How was he inviting you to partner with him?

04 Why do you think listening is a necessary step for witnessing to others in a timely and effective way?

Repeat the exercise

For this week, we invite you to repeat the exercise on page 72 or to try the reach exercise there if you have not already.

Share the Good News

We started this Practice with a simple question: What needed to happen for you to begin following a Jewish rabbi who lived almost two millennia ago? And the answer is the same for each of us: through a long chain of people who shared the good news of Jesus. Whether it was your mom, your coworker, your youth pastor, or someone else—*someone* had to share the good news for it to reach you. In today's passage, Paul brings us back to that question of *how* and invites us to close this Practice by once again considering living the same life that led us to believe the good news.

Read Romans 10v13—15.

Discuss the Scripture

01 Reflecting on this Practice, what have you noticed tends to prevent you from sharing the good news, and how has this Practice helped with that?

02 What do you find to be especially beautiful about the good news of who God is, and the life that can be found in relationship with him?

03 How has reflecting on your own personal story of coming to follow Jesus impacted your perspective or feelings toward this Practice?

04 Consider the words *everyone* and *anyone*—that *everyone* can believe and be saved, and *anyone* can be a messenger of the good news. How has this Practice made sense of both those realities for you?

Discuss the practice

01 What questions or challenges around witnessing did this Practice speak to directly?

02 Which session or exercise from this Practice was the most impactful for you personally, and why?

03 If you could share only one insight or reflection that you want to internalize going forward from this Practice, what would it be?

04 How do you want to relate to that list of three to five people you wrote down in the first session in the coming weeks and months?

Repeat the exercise

For this week, we invite you to repeat the exercise on page 92 or to try the reach exercise there if you have not already.

To inquire about ordering this Companion Guide in bulk quantities for your church, small group, or staff, contact churches@penguinrandomhouse.com.